JUV/E   Keats, Ezra Jack.
PN
6081   God is in the
.K42   mountain.
1994

$15.45

JUV/E   Keats, Ezra
PN   Jack.
6081
.K42   God is in the
1994   mountain.

$15.45

DATE	BORROWER'S NAME	

CHICAGO PUBLIC LIBRARY
SCOTTSDALE BRANCH
4101 W. 79TH ST.   60652

BAKER & TAYLOR

God is in the Mountain

God is in the Mountain

Selected and illustrated by

EZRA JACK KEATS

Henry Holt and Company
New York

Henry Holt and Company, Inc.
Publishers since 1866
115 West 18th Street
New York, New York 10011

Henry Holt is a registered
trademark of Henry Holt and Company, Inc.

Published in Canada by Fitzhenry & Whiteside Ltd.,
195 Allstate Parkway, Markham, Ontario L3R 4T8.

Library of Congress Cataloging-in-Publication Data
Keats, Ezra Jack.
God is in the mountains / selected and illustrated by
Ezra Jack Keats.
1. Quotations, English.   2. Quotations.   I. Title.
PN6081.K42   1994   200 — dc20   93-29721

ISBN 0-8050-3168-5

Revised Edition — 1994

Printed in the United States of America
on acid-free paper. ∞
1   3   5   7   9   10   8   6   4   2

This is a collection of voices and intimations.
They speak to us from different times and different places.
What they have in common is the awareness of a dimension
without which life is indeed meaningless.

I should like to share these glimpses into the Way offered us —
beautiful and potent, within us and around us, ever present and waiting.

E.J.K.

God is in the Mountain

I am in every religion as a thread
through a string of pearls.

HINDUISM

The heavens declare the glory of God . . .

JUDAISM

. . . If I am not for myself, who will be for me?
And if I am only for myself, what am I?
And if not now, when?

JUDAISM

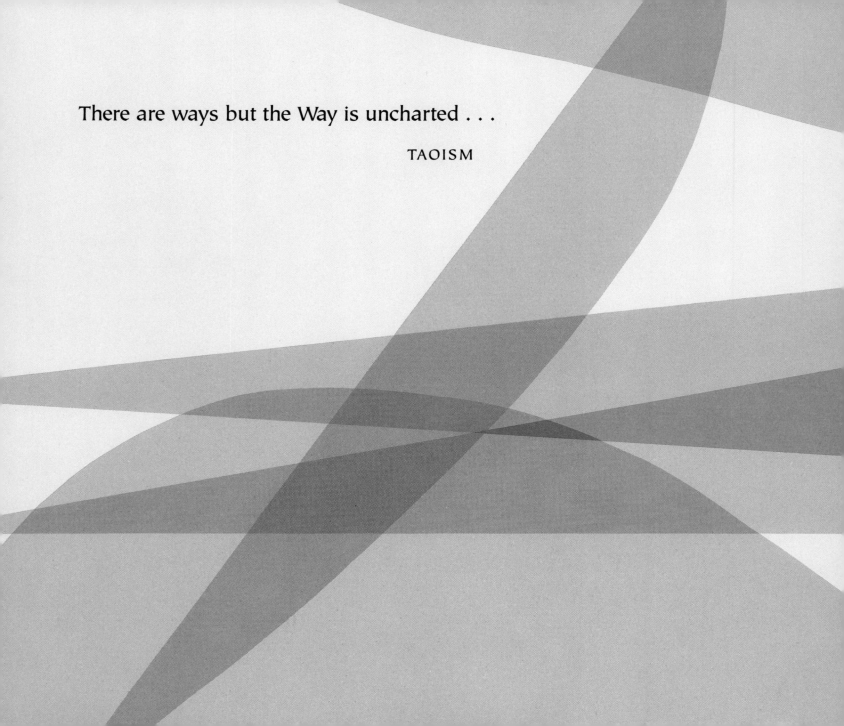

There are ways but the Way is uncharted . . .

TAOISM

The feet can walk; let them walk.
The hands can hold; let them hold.
Hear what is heard by your ears;
see what is seen by your eyes. . . .

TAOISM

. . . weave for us a garment of brightness;
May the warp be the white light of morning,
May the weft be the red light of evening,
May the fringes be the falling rain,
May the border be the standing rainbow.
Thus weave for us a garment of brightness,
That we may walk fittingly where birds sing,
That we may walk fittingly where grass is green,
O our Mother the Earth, O our Father the Sky.

AMERICAN INDIAN, TEWA PUEBLO

Are you less than a piece of earth?
When a piece of earth finds a friend, that is, the spring,
it gains a hundred thousand flowers.

ISLAM

No kind of beast is there on earth
nor fowl that flieth with its wings,
but is a folk like you . . .

ISLAM

God is in the water, God is in the dry land,
God is in the heart, God is in the forest,
God is in the mountain, God is in the cave.

SIKHISM

Being beautiful one should not be charmed by it:
it is the light of the Lord that shines in all bodies.

SIKHISM

I am like the quetzal bird,
I am created in the one and only God;
I sing sweet songs among the flowers;
I chant songs and rejoice in my heart.

AZTEC

. . . If two make peace with each other
in this one house,
they shall say to the mountain:
"Be moved," and it shall be moved.

CHRISTIANITY

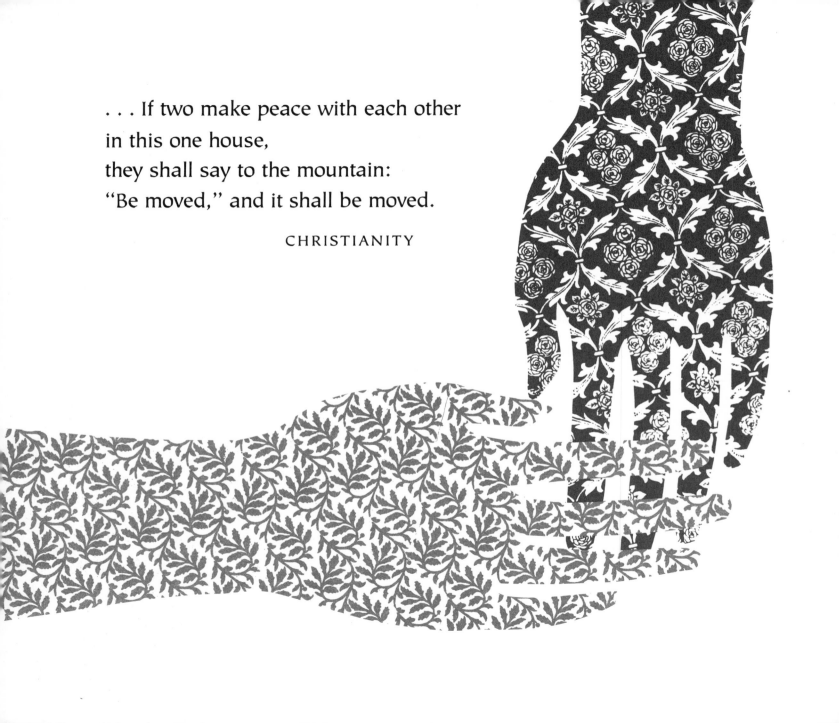

Consider the lilies of the field, how they grow;
they toil not, neither do they spin:
and yet I say unto you, that even Solomon in all his glory
was not arrayed like one of these.

CHRISTIANITY

He who is the Self in man,
and he who is the Self in the sun,
are one.

HINDUISM

What is within us is also without.
What is without is also within.
He who sees difference between
what is within and what is without
goes evermore from death to death.

HINDUISM

All ye under the heaven!
Regard heaven as your father, earth as your mother,
and all things as your brother and sisters.

SHINTOISM

The power of spiritual forces in the Universe —
how active it is everywhere!
Invisible to the eyes and impalpable to the senses,
it is inherent in all things,
and nothing can escape its operation.

CONFUCIANISM

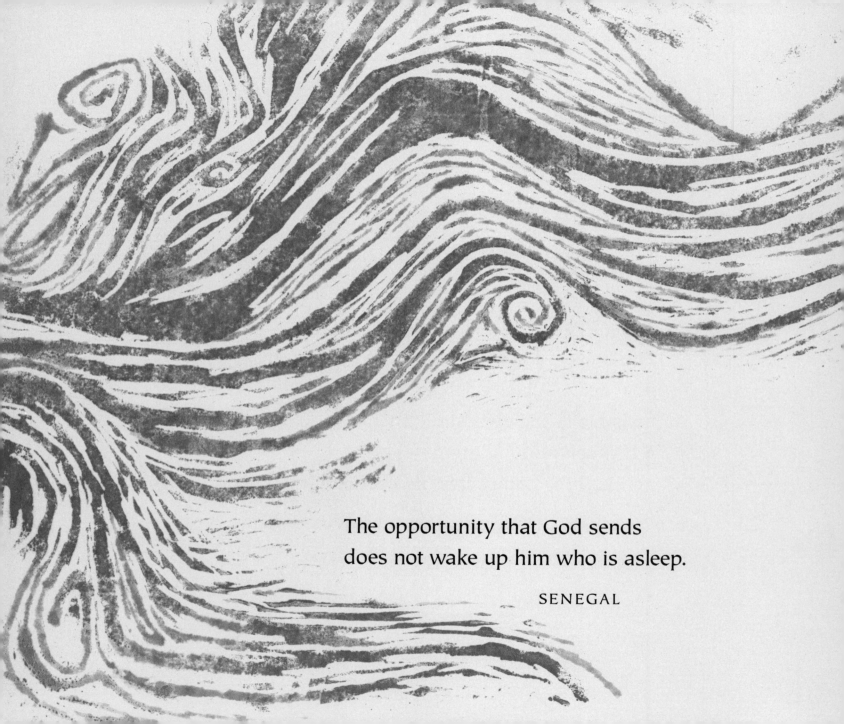

The opportunity that God sends
does not wake up him who is asleep.

SENEGAL

Talking with one another
is loving one another.

KENYA

Every divine word has come into existence
through the heart's thought and tongue's command.

EGYPTIAN

. . . And from the shining stream of rain the trees
Perfect their fruits. Joint cause of all am I.

GREEK

Mortal though I be, yea ephemeral, if but a moment
I gaze up to the night's starry domain of heaven,
Then no longer on earth I stand; I touch the Creator,
And my lively spirit drinketh immortality.

GREEK

Do you not seek a light,
ye who are surrounded by darkness?

BUDDHISM

Stars, darkness, a lamp, a phantom, dew, a bubble.
A dream, a flash of lightning, and a cloud —
thus we should look upon the world.

BUDDHISM

EZRA JACK KEATS (1916–83) was the author and illustrator of twenty-three picture books, among them *The Snowy Day,* for which he was awarded the 1963 Caldecott Medal. He was also the illustrator of thirty books by other authors. His works have been translated into seventeen languages, including Swedish, Danish, Chinese, Japanese, and Turkish.

Ezra Jack Keats's humanitarian vision continues to influence children's book writers and artists today.

Grateful acknowledgment is made to the following publishers and authors for permission to reprint copyrighted material:

Behrman House, Inc., for the following selection reprinted from SAYINGS OF THE FATHERS by Joseph H. Hertz, published by Behrman House, Inc., 1261 Broadway, New York 1, New York. ("If I am not for myself, who will be for me?" — Hillel)

E. J. Brill Ltd. for the following selection from THE GOSPEL ACCORDING TO THOMAS, ed. A. Guillaumont, H.-Ch. Puech, G. Quispel and W. Till and Yassah 'Abd al-Masih, E. J. Brill, 1959, Leiden. ("If two make peace with each other in this one house" — Jesus)

The Clarendon Press, Oxford, for the following selections from THE OXFORD BOOK OF GREEK VERSE IN TRANSLATION, ed. Higham and Bowra. ("And from the shining stream of rain . . ." — Aeschylus; "Mortal though I be . . ." — Ptolemaeus)

HarperCollins and Coward-McCann for the following selections from AMERICAN INDIAN PROSE AND POETRY by Margot Astrow, copyright © 1946 by Margot Astrow. ("I am like the quetzal bird" — A song by Nezahualcoyotl; "Weave for us a garment of brightness" — Tewa)

HarperCollins, for the following selections from THE CHOICE IS ALWAYS OURS by D. B. Phillips. ("Do you not seek a light" — The Dhammapada; "I am in every religion . . ." — Bhagavad-Gita)

Penguin USA and Russell and Volkening, Inc., for the following selection from THE MASKS OF GOD — ORIENTAL MYTHOLOGY, copyright © 1962 by Joseph Campbell. Reprinted by permission of the author. ("Every divine word has come into existence")

The Peter Pauper Press for the following selections from AFRICAN PROVERBS by C. and W. Leslau. ("The opportunity that God sends"; "Talking with one another")

Random House and the estate of Dr. S. G. Champion for the following selections from READING FROM WORLD RELIGIONS by S. G. Champion and Dorothy Short, reprinted by permission of Mrs. B. C. Briault. ("Being beautiful one should not be charmed by it" — Arjan; "God is in the water, God is in the dry land" — Gobino Sinah; "Are you less than a piece of earth?" — Mishkat-el-Massabih; "No kind of beast is there on earth" — Qur'an; "The heavens declare the glory of God . . ." — Psalms of David; "Stars, darkness, a lamp, a phantom . . ." — The Vagrakkhedika; "Consider the lilies of the field, how they grow" — Jesus; "The feet can walk, let them walk" — Chuang-tzu; "All ye under heaven" — Oracle of the deity Atsuta)

Blanche Stace for the following selection from THE TEACHINGS OF THE MYSTICS by W. T. Stace, reprinted by permission of the author. ("There are ways but the Way is uncharted . . ." — Lao-tzu)

Vedanta Society of Southern California for the following selections from the Prabhavananda-Manchester THE UPANISHADS, copyright by the Vedanta Society of California. ("What is within us is also without" — Katha; "He who is the Self in man" — Taittiriya)